appropriate guesses. In some cases there may be a correct answer (Which animal in the picture is the biggest?), and in other cases there may be different interpretations of what is happening (How do you think the boy in the green hat is feeling?).

Depending upon your child, it may be helpful to read only a part of the book at a time. It may also be helpful to read this book more than once with your child. In a second reading, consider making up some of your own questions that invite your child to count items or discuss what is happening in the scenes. Remember to praise your child's efforts and keep the interaction fun.

Try to keep these tips in mind, but don't worry about doing everything right. Simply sharing the book together will help prepare your child for reading, mathematics, and doing well in school.

How Many?

A Counting Book

A We Both Read® Book

Text Copyright © 2016 by D. J. Panec
Illustrations Copyright © 2016 by Katherine Blackmore
Reading Consultant: Bruce Johnson, M.Ed.

We Both Read® is a trademark of Treasure Bay, Inc.

Published by
Treasure Bay, Inc.
P.O. Box 119
Novato, CA 94948 USA

Printed in Malaysia

Library of Congress Catalog Card Number: 2015940398

Hardcover ISBN: 978-1-60115-291-6
Paperback ISBN: 978-1-60115-292-3

Visit us online at: www.TreasureBayBooks.com

PR 11-15

How Many?

A Counting Book

By D. J. Panec

Illustrated by Katherine Blackmore

TREASURE BAY

The beach is a wonderful place to play. How
many children do you see playing in the water?
How many are building a sand castle?

Can you guess what the weather is like here? One woman is holding an orange umbrella. Why do you think she has brought her umbrella to the beach?

Many animals live in the forest. Can you find three birds in the trees? How many birds are in the air? How many altogether?

How many deer do you see in this picture? What do you think the animals will do when the hikers get close to them?

These children enjoy watching people build. How many children are watching? How many adults are working? Can you find the number **1** on this page?

All the workers are wearing yellow hard hats. Why do you think construction workers wear those hard hats? What do you think they are building?

This is a dairy farm. How many cows do you see here? What do children often drink that comes from cows? What do you think cows eat and drink?

These cows are black and white. What kinds of
animals do you see that are all black? How many
animals do you see that are all white?

Look at all the snow! What season do you think it
is? How many children are skating? How many are
sledding down the hill?

How do you think the child in the green hat is
feeling? How about the girl in the brown skirt?
How about the boy in the red hat?

Many different kinds of fish and animals live in
the ocean. How many yellow fish can you find in
this picture? Can you find five sea stars?

How many sea stars are red? How many are orange?
Do you think sea stars are fish? What other animals
do you see that might not be fish?

Many people love the dinosaurs in the Natural
History Museum. Which dinosaur do you think is
the scariest? Which do you think is the longest
one? Which is the smallest?

How many children here are wearing green shorts? How many are wearing blue pants? Which child do you think might be in the wrong group?

Look! A parade! There are seven brass instruments
in the marching band. Four of them are trombones.
How many are trumpets? How many children are
riding bicycles?

The American flag has three colors on it. What colors do you see on the flag? Can you find the number **4** on this page? How do you think the children in the parade are feeling?

The airport is a busy place. How many people in
uniform do you see? What kind of jobs do you
think they do? Can you find the number **7** on
this page?

It looks like people are starting to board one of the airplanes. What do you think is happening with the lady with the purple suitcase? How many black suitcases do you see?

This is the Sonoran Desert. How many desert tortoises do you see here? Which cactus is the tallest? Which is the shortest? How hot do you think it is in this picture?

Do you think it is always hot in the desert? Can you find the number **4** in this picture? Look everywhere—it's a little tricky! (Is there a cactus that looks like a **4**?)

Go, team, go! Do you know what game these children are playing? Can you find the number **9** in this picture? Can you find the number **5**?

How many players are on the red team? How many players are on the blue team? How many players are there altogether?

It's pumpkin time! What season do you think it is?
What do you think the weather feels like? Can you
find the number **2** in this picture?

Some of the children are wearing scarves. How
many scarves are blue? How many are striped?
How many scarves are there altogether?

Someone is having a birthday. Can you guess whose birthday it is? How old do you think she is today? Can you find the number **6** in the picture?

The guests are wearing purple and green hats. How many green hats do you see? How many purple ones? How many children do you see at this party?

It's lunchtime! How many children are eating in the diner today? How many grown-ups? Which table has the most people? Which has the least?

Some of the children are behaving nicely. Which ones do you think are behaving nicely? Can you find the number **3** in this picture?

These dogs are enjoying a day at the dog park.
How many dogs do you see here? Which dog is
jumping the highest?

Which dog is the smallest? Which is the biggest?
Do you see any cats here? Why do you think they
are hiding?

It's a warm and rainy day in the park. What season do you think it is? How many baby birds are in the nest? How many *more* worms must the mother bird find to feed all of her babies?

How many baby ducklings are following their
mother? One duckling is going the wrong way!
Why do you think that duckling is not following
its mother?

These children are putting on a play. How many
are dressed as little kittens? Do you think these
kittens are pretending to be happy or sad?

The play is about kittens that have lost their
mittens. How many pairs of mittens do you
think they've lost? Can you find their mittens?

A farmers market is a great place to find fresh fruit and vegetables. How many different kinds of food do you see that are green?

How many kinds of food do you see that are orange? How many different apple colors do you see? What are the colors?

It's a busy time for shopping. What time of year
do you think it is? Do you think it is cold or hot?
The bike store has a striped awning over the door.

How many red stripes do you see? How many
white stripes? How do you think the young boy in
front of the bike shop is feeling?

This classroom has many fun activities to choose from. Can you name three activities the children are doing? Can you find the number **10** in this picture? Can you find the number **8**?

How many children are sitting down? How many are standing up? Who do you think is having the most fun? How do you think some of the other children are feeling?

If you liked **How Many?**, here is another
We Both Read® book you are sure to enjoy!

Too Many Cats

Suzu has asked for a white cat for her birthday.
Now, on the night before her birthday, she begins
to find cats all over the house—most of them in
very unusual colors! Suzu loves cats, but now she
has too many! Focusing on reading the names
of colors and the numbers from one to ten, this
Level PK-K book is designed for the child who is
just being introduced to reading.